ANDREW JACKSON'S
AMERICA

1824–1850

ANDREW JACKSON'S AMERICA

1824–1850

Christopher Collier
James Lincoln Collier

BENCHMARK **B**OOKS

MARSHALL CAVENDISH
NEW YORK

ACKNOWLEDGMENT: The authors wish to thank William E. Gienapp, professor of history, Harvard University, for his careful reading of the text of this volume of The Drama of American History and his thoughtful and useful comments. The work has been much improved by Professor Gienapp's notes. The authors are deeply in his debt but, of course, assume full responsibility for the substance of the work, including any errors.

Photo research by James Lincoln Collier.
COVER PHOTO: Corbis-Bettmann.
PHOTO CREDITS: The photographs in this book are used by permission and through the courtesy of: Independence National Historic Park: 10, 12, 53. Prints and Photographs Division, Library of Congress: 13, 26, 43, 66, 79. Joslyn Art Museum: 16, 28, 33 (top), 76, 80 (left), 80 (right). Abby Aldrich Rockefeller Folk Art Center: 20, 31, 47, 68. Colonial Williamsburg Foundation: 22. Corbis-Bettmann: 33 (bottom), 34, 36, 41, 45, 48 (top), 48 (bottom), 55, 57, 59, 60, 63, 67, 69. National Museum of American Art: 81, 82, 85.

Benchmark Books
Marshall Cavendish Corporation
99 White Plains Road
Tarrytown, New York 10591-9001

©1999 Christopher Collier and James Lincoln Collier

Library of Congress Cataloging-in-Publication Data

Collier, Christopher, date
Andrew Jackson's America, 1824–1850 / Christopher Collier, James Lincoln Collier.
p. cm.   —(Drama of American history)
Includes bibliographical references and index.
Summary: Examines the events and personalities, particularly President Andrew Jackson, that shaped the development of the United States during the first half of the nineteenth century.
ISBN 0-7614-0779-0 (lib. bdg.)
1. United States—History—1815–1861—Juvenile literature. 2. United States—Politics and government—1815–1861—Juvenile literature. 3. Jackson, Andrew, 1767–1845—Juvenile literature.
[1. United States—History—1815–1861. 2. United States—Politics and government—1815–1861.
3. Jackson, Andrew , 1767–1845.]
I. Collier, James Lincoln, date. II. Title. III. Series: Collier, Christopher, date, Drama of American history.
E338.C84 1998
973.5'6–dc21   97-30546
                                CIP
                                AC

Printed in Italy

1 3 5 6 4 2

CONTENTS

PREFACE

Over many years of both teaching and writing for students at all levels, from grammar school to graduate school, it has been borne in on us that many, if not most, American history textbooks suffer from trying to include everything of any moment in the history of the nation. Students become lost in a swamp of factual information, and as a consequence lose track of how those facts fit together and why they are significant and relevant to the world today.

In this series, our effort has been to strip the vast amount of available detail down to a central core. Our aim is to draw in bold strokes, providing enough information, but no more than is necessary, to bring out the basic themes of the American story, and what they mean to us now. We believe that it is surely more important for students to grasp the underlying concepts and ideas that emerge from the movement of history, than to memorize an array of facts and figures.

The difference between this series and many standard texts lies in what has been left out. We are convinced that students will better remember the important themes if they are not buried under a heap of names, dates, and places.

In this sense, our primary goal is what might be called citizenship education. We think it is critically important for America as a nation and Americans as individuals to understand the origins and workings of the public institutions that are central to American society. We have asked ourselves again and again what is most important for citizens of our democracy to know so they can most effectively make the system work for them and the nation. For this reason, we have focused on political and institutional history, leaving social and cultural history less well developed.

This series is divided into volumes that move chronologically through the American story. Each is built around a single topic, such as the Pilgrims, the Constitutional Convention, or immigration. Each volume has been written so that it can stand alone, for students who wish to research a given topic. As a consequence, in many cases material from previous volumes is repeated, usually in abbreviated form, to set the topic in its historical context. That is to say, students of the Constitutional Convention must be given some idea of relations with England, and why the Revolution was fought, even though the material was covered in detail in a previous volume. Readers should find that each volume tells an entire story that can be read with or without reference to other volumes.

Despite our belief that it is of the first importance to outline sharply basic concepts and generalizations, we have not neglected the great dramas of American history. The stories that will hold the attention of students are here, and we believe they will help the concepts they illustrate to stick in their minds. We think, for example, that knowing of Abraham Baldwin's brave and dramatic decision to vote with the small states at the Constitutional Convention will bring alive the Connecticut Compromise, out of which grew the American Senate.

Each of these volumes has been read by esteemed specialists in its particular topic; we have benefited from their comments.

CHAPTER I

A Man for an Age

The period of American history from 1820 to around 1845 or 1850 has been called by many historians the Age of Jackson. In fact, Andrew Jackson was president of the United States only from 1829 to 1837, and his influence in politics dwindled after he retired from office. But for some thirty years, he was seen by many Americans as the greatest hero of their times. He had been a victorious general, winning glory in battle. He had been an important figure in politics for many years before he actually became president. He had a commanding personality, a strong belief in his own ideas, and the ability to make things go his way. He seemed to many Americans admirable in all ways.

He seemed so because he matched the spirit of the times. These were new and different times in America, and people were looking for a new and different kind of hero. Only a generation earlier, Americans had admired people like George Washington, a man of shining character who always put the good of the nation ahead of his own; Benjamin Franklin, brilliant scientist, clever writer, astute diplomat; Thomas Jefferson, philosopher and visionary determined to build a great nation on the North American continent.

Andrew Jackson's strength and determination are clearly visible on his face. Jackson considered himself a "man of the people," but the rather imperial pose chosen by the artist is suggestive of his powerful personality.

Andrew Jackson was different—a tough, forceful man. In this respect he was like Washington, more concerned with getting results than with intellectual subtleties; but very unlike Washington, willing to brush aside ethical questions, and even the law, to do what he thought had to be done. Jackson was exactly the sort of man to appeal to Americans of his day.

Historians today, for the most part, do not like the so-called Great Man theory of history. They believe that things do not happen simply because kings, generals, presidents want them to happen. They say instead that unpredictable circumstances, like famines, migrations, technological developments, and similar events are most important in shaping history. We shall see in this chapter how the invention of the steamboat and the arrival of millions of Europeans dramatically altered the American situation. Historians also believe that events may also be shaped by ideas and beliefs which catch people up and urge them on to this or that course: many of the first white settlers came to America because of their ideas about how they believed God wanted them to live.

We have to be careful, therefore, when we ascribe events to the work of great men. Nonetheless, the character of leaders does matter. Historians agree that without George Washington—or somebody very like him—in charge of the army during the Revolution, there never would have been a United States. Similarly, as we shall see, if we had had a different sort of person from Andrew Jackson as president in the 1830s, many things would have turned out differently.

How, then, were Americans changing after 1820 that made a man like Jackson seem so admirable to so many of them? We must begin by understanding that throughout most of history the vast majority of human beings have lived in tightly controlled despotisms ruled by princes, kings, or emperors, in which only a tiny minority of aristocrats had many rights at all. Ordinary people in many cases were not even allowed to leave the estate of the lord they worked for to find a better job. They certainly did not vote for their rulers or have any say in how the laws were written. Often they could be imprisoned or even executed by powerful rulers on a whim. In fact, many millions of people in the world still live in such despotisms.

Despotic systems did not rule everybody, however. People living in small hunting-and-gathering societies, like the North American Indians, often had rough democracies and a good deal of freedom. But in the large societies, few people were in any sense free.

That slowly began to change during the three or four centuries leading up to the European discovery of America. In England especially, ordinary people started slowly to gain some rights and liberties. When the English began to colonize America in the 1600s, they brought with them the idea that they ought to have certain rights. These rights gradually expanded and were finally set down in our justly celebrated Bill of Rights, which was modeled in part on similar English documents. (Readers who want to know more about the Bill of Rights and the founding of the United States can consult *Creating the Constitution* in this series, *The Drama of American History.*)

The United States, in 1789, when George Washington was sworn in as the first president, was a vastly freer country then most nations in the world. It was nonetheless what historians call a *deferential* society, in which ordinary people deferred to the ideas of the wealthy and more powerful. Most Americans, high, low, and in between, believed that God had arranged it that some people would lead and some would follow. They believed quite honestly that the "better people" ought to rule, for they would have "better" ideas about how things ought to be done. Even Washington himself, when he was president, said openly that once the people had chosen their leaders, they ought to follow them without argument.

By 1820, however, the deferential society was being pushed aside. A new idea was growing, that "every man is

In the colonial period and the early years of the new nation, American society was "deferential." George Washington said flatly that once Americans had chosen their leaders, they should follow their advice.

as good as the next." It is always difficult to see exactly how an idea like this one—often referred to as "egalitarianism"—came forward, but we can find some of the causes in those changing circumstances we spoke of a little while back. One such change was a dramatic growth in the population of the nation. Some of this population increase came from immigration. Throughout most of the nineteenth century, there were no bars against newcomers; anyone could come to America who wanted to. There were plenty of reasons for them to come. In Germany there had been revolutions, followed by government clampdowns. In many parts of Europe from time to time there were food shortages. Unemployment was common, and in most European countries ordinary people had few of the freedoms Americans had gained. Rooting oneself up, saying good-bye forever to old friends, aging fathers and mothers, and the old familiar vil-

This picture, from a contemporary publication, shows families leaving the Swiss city of Basel for America in 1805.

lage was always hard, but to many Europeans it seemed worth it, and they came by the hundreds of thousands: in the 1820s, over 150,000; in the 1830s, 600,000; in the 1840s, 1.5 million.

Nonetheless, despite this huge immigration, most of the population growth in the United States at the time was due to natural fertility. American families were having lots of children. Families with four or five children were commonplace, and families with eight or ten were not unusual. Indeed, families with as many as twenty children could be found. Furthermore, children in America were more likely to survive childhood than children in many other places: Americans usually had enough food and, living in the open countryside, were less likely to catch contagious diseases. As a result, in the 1830s a *third* of all Americans were under the age of ten.

After 1830, family size began to drop, but was still large by comparison with today. In total, the population grew a third every ten years and doubled every twenty-three years. (By comparison, it took from 1930 to 1990 for the population to double.)

Three of the four children of George and Lydia Slater, of Webster, Massachusetts. American children suffered less from disease and malnutrition than many children elsewhere; three of the four Slater children survived to grow up, a higher ratio than in the past, but becoming common in nineteenth-century North America.

This population growth was proportionally greater in American cities than in the countryside, especially in the seacoast ports like New York, Boston, and Philadelphia. Immigrants in particular tended to settle in cities and work there as laborers and craftspeople or in small mills and factories. But in the 1830s, about 80 percent of Americans lived on farms. Land had to be found for all these new people; and after they had gobbled up all the land in the area where they were born, they pushed west to cut new farms out of the forests, felling trees with axes, breaking the ground with plow and ox, building houses with hammers, saws, hand drills, chisels.

These new Americans, especially the ones in the new western lands, with no landlord or boss to answer to, were more independent than virtually any other group of people in the world. Indeed, in certain respects these largely self-sufficient farmers were more independent than most Americans are today, for reasons we shall look at shortly. A farm family growing its own food, making its own clothes from wool from its own sheep, and selling a little extra produce—a few bushels of wheat, of apples—for a little cash for their taxes and to buy an ax or a pair of scissors, were really beholden to nobody. On top of it, out in the hinterlands there were far fewer of the rich and mighty to be deferred to than there were in the old cities and towns along the East Coast, some of which by Jackson's day were nearly two hundred years old.

The open frontier was not the only reason why egalitarian ideas were catching on in America. During the Revolution of the 1770s, American leaders in the fight against Britain talked and wrote a great deal about equality—"inalienable rights," as the Declaration of Independence put it. Later, when the people were voting to accept the Constitution in 1787 and 1788, there was a great deal of talk about the Bill of Rights. Many of the leaders had been using terms like "inalienable rights" in the abstract, in order to make a case for breaking away from England. But by the 1820s, people had come to believe that such terms meant exactly

Americans living on farms and in villages, like Bethlehem, Pennsylvania, were self-supporting and quite independent. This picture was painted on the spot by Karl Bodmer, a Swiss painter who traveled through the United States in the 1830s

what they said—that everybody had certain rights, and that each person was as good as the next. The people themselves were making theories of liberty concrete. During the Age of Jackson, America was becoming more and more democratic.

It is not surprising that Andrew Jackson became a hero to many Americans. Born in South Carolina in 1767, he was not, like Washington, Jefferson, and many of the Founding Fathers, an aristocrat living in a grand house with many servants. He was instead a country boy, raised to rough country ways among rough country people. He was, nonetheless, ambitious. At the age of about thirteen, he fought briefly in the American Revolution. He went on to study law when the Revolution was over. He settled in Tennessee, one of those frontier places filling up with new people. Like many lawyers, he ran for public office, becoming a representative in the U.S. Congress, a senator, and finally a judge on the Tennessee supreme court. A fiery man, he fought several duels, in one of which he killed his opponent.

The Americans flooding over the Appalachians to the western lands were inevitably in conflict with the Indians who had been there first. There was frequent fighting between the two peoples. As a major general in the Tennessee militia, Jackson defeated the Creeks in battles in 1813 and 1814. The War of 1812 was on. Jackson was commissioned a major general in the United States Army, and, in 1815, he defeated a large British force in the Battle of New Orleans before news of the peace treaty ending the war had come across the Atlantic. (For the story of the War of 1812 see the eighth volume in this series, *The Jeffersonian Republicans*.) In 1818, Jackson led troops against the Seminole Indians in Florida, which was legally Spanish territory. He executed two British citizens living there for inciting the Creeks against the Americans, something he had no legal right to do. Nonetheless, when the United States acquired Florida by treaty, Jackson was appointed the military governor of the territory.

Jackson was now in his late fifties. From modest beginnings he became a war hero, a senator, a judge. It should now be clear why he had such appeal for all those new Americans breaking out of the deferential attitudes many of their forebears had held.

One endearing trait, then, was his egalitarianism—his belief that anyone could rise from lowly circumstances to become anything he wanted to become, even president, as Jackson himself aspired to do. He was truly "a man of the people," who had been born and raised among ordinary farmers, and despite his growing eminence, he never forgot where he had come from. This was a new kind of leader. Presidents Washington,

Jefferson, and Madison would have been insulted if you had called them men of the people; Jackson took pride in the idea.

Jackson was, like the frontier people pushing over the mountains to build new lives, aggressive, determined to push ahead, get things done, even if it meant ignoring moral or legal questions, as he had done when he went into Spanish Florida to chastise the Seminoles.

Jackson had arisen in the West and personified what Americans saw as frontier characteristics: rose from not much to something very great without aristocratic ancestors or much formal education—a self-made man; he was a man of action who took matters into his own hands and often opted for violent solutions to problems he faced; he was concerned about hard reality rather than philosophies and theories; his great aims as president were to expand the frontier, develop the West, and make sure that every white man—not just the wealthy with friends in high places—got an equal chance in life and equal benefit from the government. For Americans, he symbolized opportunity, self-reliance, and success. Andrew Jackson personified the aspirations of the restless, striving millions of common folk.

CHAPTER II

The Industrial Revolution Comes to America

Andrew Jackson, as we shall see, would prove to be a forceful and domineering president who would make his imprint on America. But he was not by himself responsible for the changes that swept over the nation during the time that has been named for him. As ever, there were forces moving on their own which Jackson could no more control than he could control the moon and the tides.

One of these forces of change was industrialization. To repeat what we have earlier seen, in 1820, 80 percent of Americans still lived as independent farmers, growing much of what they needed and producing just a little extra for the market. Only a very small percentage of Americans worked in factories and mills, because there were very few factories and mills for them to work in. To be sure, some Americans worked in small crafts shops making barrels, cobbling shoes, blacksmithing. Others were sailors and fishermen; still others worked in city stores and shops. But these were a small minority.

A key point about the preindustrial era is that most things were made one at a time, by hand. A gunsmith would make each part for the particular gun he was working on; parts made for one gun would not usually fit another one. And this was true in most places in the world.

But in Europe, and especially in England, which many Americans still took as a model for many things, the industrial revolution had already begun by the late 1700s. For two hundred years, England had been growing rich and powerful with the help of its colonies. These colonies were producing all sorts of raw materials, most of which—like cotton, tobacco, hides, timber, minerals—went to England. Indeed, the American colonies had once been part of this vast economic empire, contributing to British wealth.

Black slaves saw logs to be split by hand into shingles for houses. Before industrialization, most things were made laboriously by hand in this fashion. This sketch was part of a series about everyday life in Virginia drawn by an amateur artist, Lewis Miller, probably in the 1850s.

But this wealth depended upon turning all that raw material into finished goods—cotton and wool into sheets and trousers, hides into shoes and boots, timber into furniture and ships. These things could be made by hand as they had been for centuries, but demand for them was great, and it was clear that anyone who could produce them by machines could get rich. Inventors took up the challenge.

One of the key inventions was the development of a practical steam engine by the Englishman James Watt in 1769. The new device freed factories from dependence on waterwheels for power and allowed them to be built in cities where there was good transportation and no shortage of labor. By the time George Washington became our first president, industry was booming in England and in other places in Europe. Later, steam power would be applied to ships and carriages to create the steamboat and the railway train.

The virtues of industry seemed clear to many Americans. Alexander Hamilton, the first secretary of the treasury, was particularly eager to see the new United States develop a strong industrial system. Why pay the British to make cloth and tables out of American cotton and timber, when Americans could do it themselves? George Washington agreed with Hamilton and supported various plans to encourage manufacturing in the United States. (For an explanation of Hamilton's policies see *Building a New Nation* in this series.)

But not everybody was so-minded. In particular, Thomas Jefferson was convinced that the greatness of America lay in the people who worked the soil. These independent farm families, who made their own soap, shirts, candles, cider, and much else, were not beholden to landlords, employers, or anyone else. Jefferson had spent time in Europe. He had seen the mills there, with their underpaid workers in rags toiling fourteen hours a day in dirty factories; he had seen the slums in which most of them lived. He believed that cities were bad and factories were worse—though both, he allowed, were often a necessary evil. Let the

Throughout the early history of America, a great proportion of the lives of women was spent at the spinning wheel, making yarn which could be woven into cloth. Housewives and their daughters would spend day after day spinning, especially in winter.

English have them; Americans would be a happy and prosperous people living country lives and selling their produce to the unfortunate city dwellers abroad.

But Jefferson was not to have his way. Hamilton's various schemes to promote industry did not always work, but his idea that industry ought to be promoted carried. As the War of 1812 wound down in 1815, a new set of leaders, pushing the New Nationalism, were taking over. These men, among them John Quincy Adams, Henry Clay, John C. Calhoun, and Daniel Webster, wanted to see a great and prosperous nation bound together by an active and growing system of commerce. Among other things, they favored a protective tariff, that is to say, a high tax or duty on goods entering the United States. Such tariffs had originally been meant simply to raise money for the government—there was no income tax at that time and would not be one for decades. But the new leaders wanted to use tariffs to keep out foreign competition. For example, the British, with their superior manufacturing techniques, might be able to sell a yard of cotton cloth for five shillings—say, sixty-five cents—while a less efficient

American maker might have to charge seventy-five cents for it. But a protective tariff of, say, twelve cents would make the British item more expensive than the American one by adding the tariff duty to the cost of the item.

One of the first industries to develop in England was textiles—the making of cloth for clothes, sheets, flags, curtains, napkins, and so much else. Cloth is so plentiful today, we forget that it is one of the most basic of human necessities. Humans have always devoted almost as much time to making clothing as they have to getting food. For centuries, inventors had hunted for better ways to make cloth but had not got much farther than the spinning wheel and the handloom. Then, in 1769, Richard Arkwright invented a practical mechanical spinning jenny designed to be powered by horses, but immediately adapted to water power. Very quickly a textile industry was founded in England.

The English, however, were in no hurry to make this, or their other machines, available to people of other nations. For them the road to vast wealth was to import raw materials, like cotton, turn it into cloth, and sell the cloth back to the very people they had bought the cotton from, such as the Americans. They had strict rules against exporting any sort of machinery—indeed, they would not even allow their mill workers to emigrate.

But in 1789, a young Englishman who had been apprenticed to a spinning mill slipped out of England by claiming he was a farmer. His name was Samuel Slater. He found backers in Rhode Island and built the first American spinning mill there. Very quickly his business expanded, until he was head of one of the largest industrial empires in America. Others imitated his success, and between 1800 and 1830 the number of spindles in cotton textile factories increased from 2,000 to 1,140,000, creating a huge industry, fed by the vast cotton fields of the Deep South.

These early American textile mills were powered by waterwheels and had to be out in the countryside where there was open land alongside

Samuel Slater's cotton-spinning mill in Pawtucket, Rhode Island, set the United States on the path to industrialization. The mill was run by water power, as were most early mills, and had to be situated in the countryside. When steam power came in, mills could be built in cities, where there was good transportation and an ample supply of labor.

streams and rivers. That made it difficult to find enough workers close at hand to staff the mills, since workers had to be within easy walking distance. Slater solved the problem by putting up housing and creating little villages around the mills. Some of these villages had their own blacksmith shops, cobblers, churches, and even garden plots where food was grown for the workers. Although some people hired themselves out to work in Slater's mills as workers do today, more frequently the head of a household, usually the father, who was often a full-time farmer, would hire out some, or even all, of his family for a certain period. Many very young children worked in the mills. The father would collect the wages for the whole family and often check to see that his family members were being properly treated by the bosses.

A different system for the workers was devised by Francis Cabot Lowell for his mills in what became the town of Lowell, Massachusetts. Lowell mainly hired young women, even girls, from New England farms. These girls were housed in dormitories belonging to the mills, where they were carefully supervised so they would remain healthy and not get into trouble. Some of the girls in these dorms started their own magazines, put on plays and other entertainment for themselves. These novel labor arrangements disappeared as steam power replaced waterwheels, for the mills could then be situated in towns and cities, where there were many working people within easy walking distance.

But Americans were not just borrowing technologies from Europe. They were also inventing their own machines and systems. One of the most important of these was the cotton "gin" (short for en*gine*), invented by Eli Whitney in 1793, just as Samuel Slater was getting his cotton spinning mills going. There were two types of cotton being grown in the South: a long-fibered type that would only grow on a string of islands off the South Carolina and Georgia coasts, and a short-fibered type that would grow inland in the warm climate of the lower South. However, it was much more difficult to get the sticky seeds out of the short-fibered type; it took a person a day to clean a pound of cotton.

Whitney's cotton gin, a simple machine that rolled a comb through the cotton, made it possible for one person to clean fifty pounds of cotton a day. Very quickly farmers all over the lower South began switching to cotton. The new spinning and weaving machines in both England and America were able to process vast amounts of raw cotton. The cotton gin, combined with textile machinery, thus created a huge industry and great wealth for mill owners and families with large plantations.

An artist's sketch of an early cotton gin being worked by black slaves. The cotton gin sped up the cleaning of cotton and allowed the textile industry to boom.

Eli Whitney never made much money from his cotton gin—the machine was simple and easy to copy. But he got a contract from the U.S. government to produce ten thousand rifles for the army. Previously, guns, like almost everything else, were turned out by hand one at a time. Whitney saw that if you could make identical gun parts by machine, you could vastly speed up the manufacturing process. This was the basis of *mass production*, in which *interchangeable* parts could be swiftly assembled into a gun identical to the next one. This idea seems obvious today, but it was not so obvious in those days, when each part was handcrafted to fit a particular gun.

The advantages of mass production were clear and were quickly applied to other products. Simeon North, at the same time as Whitney was making muskets, manufactured pistols, and then Chauncey Jerome and others began making clocks by this method. Soon clocks, once owned only by the rich, were hanging on walls in simple farmhouses all over America.

It might not seem at a casual look that the creation of cheap clocks and mass-produced clothing would have momentous effects on a nation. But just as a stone thrown into a pond sends ripples across to the other side, so did this new technology begin a massive shift in the way Americans worked—indeed in how they lived their lives.

Consider textiles. Previously, millions of farm women spent a great deal of their time spinning wool or cotton into thread or yarn, weaving the yarn into cloth, and cutting and sewing the cloth into shirts, dresses, and everything else the family needed. This long, time-consuming process was central to the daily lives of American women and the girls who learned how to spin at their mothers' sides. Indeed, unmarried women were called "spinsters," so much were their lives centered around the spinning wheel.

Suddenly, within a generation, a vast amount of cheap machine-made cloth became available. Women no longer had to put in those long, tedious hours at looms and spinning wheels. In order to use their time productively, many of them began working in textile mills, like the ones owned by Slater and Lowell. Indeed, it was not long before the old home-spun fabric became a mark of poverty, or at least of a countrified lack of style. People could now buy inexpensive but better-quality textiles of brightly colored patterns impossible to weave on the home loom. Though other mass-produced goods were usually of lesser quality than handmade ones, they were much cheaper and therefore available to many more fam-

All over the United States, in small towns and big cities, Americans were producing vast quantities of raw materials, like the timber and bales of cotton seen in this painting of the little town of New Mexico, on the Mississippi, painted by Karl Bodmer in the 1830s.

ilies. Slowly but surely over the whole of the 1800s, a nation of farmers became a nation of industrial workers, laboring in factories, manufacturing textiles, tools, furniture, pots, pans, sieves, and all the rest of it.

The development of cheap clocks had similar long-term effects. In earlier days, when only the rich could afford clocks, most Americans told time by the sun, the moon, and the stars. People arranged to meet at "first light," or "at sundown." But an industrial system cannot be run efficiently if everybody arrives at the factory gates according to their own ideas of when "first light" comes. It needs to run "like clockwork." Cheap clocks now made it possible for all those girls working in the

Slater and Lowell mills to get to work on time, and every factory was topped by a bell tower that ordered every worker's daily schedule. The clocks had another subtle but serious effect on how people lived. Under the old system of "sun time," people did not cut their days up into carefully timed sections as we do today—eight hours for work, eight hours for sleep, and so on. Instead, they lived according to the season, the weather, the nature of the job. In haying season, when the hay had to be brought in fast during a dry spell, the whole family might work until midnight by moonlight. In the short days of winter, when there was less work to do, they might spend time visiting with friends and relatives. People moved more to the rhythm of nature than they do today, when our lives are often dictated by the clock. Most Americans have believed that the prosperity produced by the industrial system is worth the price of being regimented by the clock; but there have always been some Americans who have argued that the older way was better.

CHAPTER III

The New Transportation System

By the 1830s and 1840s, the industrial revolution was well under way in the United States, throwing off all sorts of factory-made products. But the industrial system would not have developed nearly as quickly had it not been for the application of the new technologies to yet another major area of life, transportation—that is, the movement of people and things from one place to another.

The United States was a vast country in 1830, ten times the size of such European powers as France and Spain, and before another generation passed it would become even larger with the addition of Texas, California, and the Pacific Northwest.

Furthermore, it was divided by two long, rugged mountain chains: the Appalachians about a hundred miles inland from the Atlantic coast, and the Rockies acting as a barrier to the Pacific coast. Roads were hard to build and were usually heavily rutted and feet deep in mud during the spring rains. Wagons were often forced to ford streams, which could be dangerous at flood times. As a result, transportation was mainly by water—up and down the coast in sailing vessels, or through the vast river systems, like the Ohio and its tributaries which ran into the Mississippi and thence down to New Orleans and the Gulf of Mexico. River transport was slow: it took six weeks for a keelboat to travel from Pittsburgh to New Orleans, and the return journey against the current took seventeen weeks or more. Early manufacturers like Slater often found that it took months for their goods to reach some markets and for the money to come back to them.

The first dramatic change in transportation was signaled in 1787 when an inventive mechanic named John Fitch demonstrated a boat powered by steam. It did not catch on, although Fitch ran a steamboat service on the Delaware River for a while. The steamboat boom began in 1807 when Robert Fulton, with an improved version, began regular service on the Hudson River between New York City and Albany. Other

Traveling over rough roads by coach was tiring and at times dangerous when there were swollen rivers to cross. Here, a coach is poled across a river on a ferry, a time-consuming operation which would be repeated many times on a long journey. This is another sketch of Virginia life by Lewis Miller.

enterprising men leaped in to provide competing steamboat lines, and soon steamboats were everywhere. One important fact about the steamboats is that they could travel *upstream* almost as easily as down.

In 1817, there were seventeen steamboats operating on the Mississippi system. By 1820, there were sixty-nine, and the number kept on soaring. Now all those cheap clocks, guns, and bolts of cloth being manufactured in the Northeast could be shipped quickly all over the United States. On their return journeys, these steamboats would bring back western wheat, whiskey, beef, lumber, and other products of the farm and forest.

But there were many areas of the nation that were some distance from a good river system, as for example western Pennsylvania and New York. Artificial rivers, or canals, had been in use in Europe for centuries, but most of them were short, like the canals that weave through cities like Venice, Amsterdam, and Copenhagen. Americans had done some canal building earlier—George Washington had once canoed up the Potomac River into the mountains to see if there was a way to build a canal to the Ohio territory on the other side. But by 1816, there were only a hundred miles of canals in the United States, the longest of them twenty-eight miles.

One of the main difficulties with building a canal was that most land was not level, but sloped, in some places for hundreds of miles. Canals had to be raised by a series of locks, which acted like water steps.

In about 1816, it occurred to Governor De Witt Clinton of New York that he could vastly enhance the wealth of his state if he could build a canal connecting the Hudson River to the Great Lakes. The Great Lakes were already linked to the Mississippi River by portage from the Illinois River. (They were connected after 1833 by canal to the Ohio River.) With a canal to Lake Erie, goods arriving in New York City could flow west to the Great Lakes, to the vast rich, agricultural hinterland of the Midwest. Similarly, western beef, wheat, and corn could flow back to *(right) By the 1830s, steamboats were traveling everywhere there was water. In this painting by Karl Bodmer, the steamboat* Napoleon *pulls up to a bank to take on passengers and freight.*

(below) Canals employed locks to raise and lower ships as the terrain sloped. Here, the lock keepers are pushing open the gates to let out water, so the level in the lock will be low enough to allow the boat to enter. Once the boat is in the lock, the gates will be closed and gates at the other end of the lock will be opened to allow the water to rise again, lifting the boat to the next level.

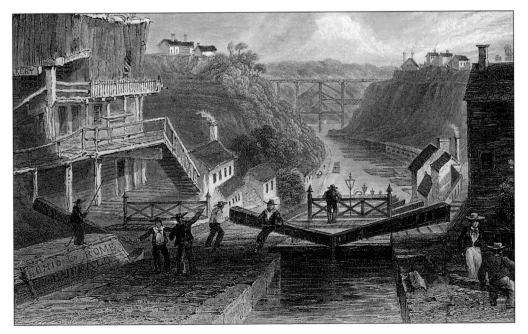

New York. New York merchants, farmers, manufacturers, importers' and consumers would all benefit.

The idea of building the Erie Canal, as it came to be called, seemed like a wild dream. But in the Age of Jackson, Americans were ready to pursue wild dreams. In the American spirit, Clinton's engineers devised an array of special equipment and got the job done. By 1825, thousands upon thousands of tons of goods were flowing along the 365 miles of the Erie Canal which was linked to the Hudson River system. Before, it had cost nineteen cents per mile to ship a ton of goods from Buffalo to New York City; through the canal it cost less than three cents a ton. Towns and cities sprang up along the canal, and very soon New York City became one of the world's busiest ports. In time, the city would supplant Boston and Philadelphia as the nation's greatest commercial center. New York City remains America's leader in business, information, and the media, because of its wonderful harbor and the head start it got from the Erie Canal.

The Erie Canal proved the immense value of canals and helped to make New York City a great center of commerce. In this drawing of 1842, we can see horses on the canal bank at left tugging the boat along.

The great success of the Erie Canal encouraged other promoters to build canals elsewhere, and by 1840 there were 3,300 miles of canals in the United States. To be sure, many canal schemes foundered, costing state governments and private investors huge sums. By 1850, the railroads were taking over anyway, and the canals were falling into disuse. But for a generation, the canals played a crucially important role in helping the industrial revolution get going.

The idea of using steam power to drive a carriage or a wagon was an obvious one, and in 1804, even before Fulton demonstrated his steamboat, a steam locomotive was developed in England. Americans, concentrating on canals, did not build significant railroads until the 1830s. The first lines were short, frequently put up to connect two nearby canals. But by the 1840s, there were several thousand miles of track running hither and thither through woods and fields. Soon, city fathers saw that they must have a railroad connection if they were to keep up in the race for wealth, and railroads continued to grow.

Coming along a little later was a parallel technology, which meshed into the rapidly growing industrial system and made it much more efficient. This was a revolution in communications. Through most of the Age of Jackson, the only way to get news from one place to another was by mail. And while the postal system had gradually gotten more speedy, with fast riders carrying the mail from city to city, it still took days or even weeks for letters to travel from one part of America to another. Thus, it might take weeks for Samuel Slater or Francis Lowell in New England to find the best price for cotton in Georgia, and weeks more for his order to go out.

This was all about to change. In 1844, Samuel F. B. Morse constructed an experimental telegraph line from Washington to Baltimore. The telegraph could not transmit sounds, only an electric current that clicked a key at the other end. Morse worked out his "Morse code" based on combinations of short and long clicks to indicate letters. Trained operators were able to send messages very rapidly by Morse code over telegraph lines. By 1852, there were twenty-three thousand miles of telegraph lines linking American cities. Now Lowell and Slater could get news of cotton prices overnight and send orders for cotton out the next day. Indeed, exchanging prices was the main use of the telegraph in its earliest days.

The telegraph had many other effects. For example, it allowed railroads to quickly coordinate their schedules to prevent trains coming from opposite directions from crashing on the single lines that were common. It enabled newspapers to print stories about events occurring a thousand miles away in the next day's papers. Americans had always been great newspaper readers, but the news they got from them was often days, if not weeks, old. Now they could get exciting news while it was fresh, and the basis was laid for the vast media system that occupies so much of our time today.

We can now see how technology made enormous changes in American life in the Age of Jackson—changes that had little to do with who happened to be president. The steamboat, the spinning jenny, interchangeable parts, the cotton gin, and other inventions working together

Early railroad trains were small and simple compared to ones developed later. Here is the famous locomotive Tom Thumb in a race against a horse-drawn wagon, which was meant to demonstrate the superiority of steam.

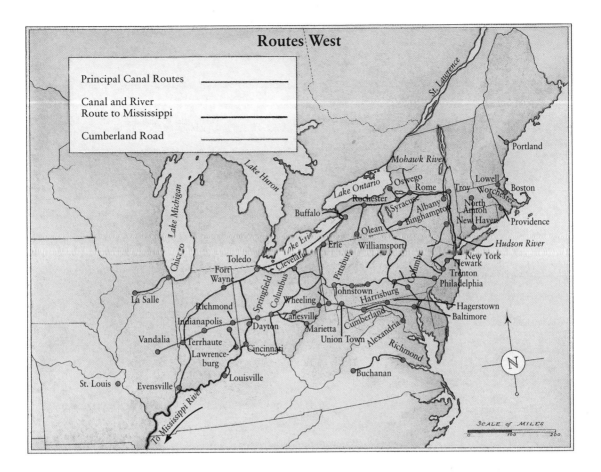

Routes West

Principal Canal Routes

Canal and River
Route to Mississippi

Cumberland Road

produced the first flush of what would in time become the world's great-est industrial economy. In five years in the early 1840s, the production of iron, essential for making machinery, was up 300 percent. Anthracite coal production, necessary for making steam, was up ten times and ship-building up 2.5 times.

But there was more to it than technology. Just as important were *ideas*—the ideas of boldness and adventure that were personified by Andrew Jackson. One observer reported that in America there was an "almost universal ambition to get forward." That was the America of Jackson: don't be held back by tradition, don't play it safe, always look for the new path, the better way. To many Americans the very idea that a thing "had always been done that way" was a good enough reason to change it. It was the future that mattered, not the past. Ideas, indeed, have power: without the idea that change itself was good, the old, traditional, rural America might have lived on much longer, even into the twentieth century, and the United States would be much different today.

The revolutions in industry, transportation, and communication also helped speed up one of Americans' great traditional activities—their unusual habit of moving from place to place with a frequency greater than that of any other people on Earth.

Of course, Americans had been moving west since they first began settling the continent. But the development of roads and canals over and around the Appalachian Mountains accelerated the process. Everywhere, people were on the move. The population of states like Ohio, Indiana, Wisconsin, Illinois exploded: for example, between 1820 and 1840, the population of Ohio tripled, that of Indiana increased fourfold.

The Erie Canal and steamboats on the Great Lakes made it possible to travel from Massachusetts to Michigan for ten dollars. "Travelers might complain of overcrowded canal boats, poor food, and swarming mosquitoes," wrote one historian, "but they were nevertheless able to travel cheaply, take their household goods with them, and be sure of reaching their destination without losing a wagon in a mudhole."

Almost as astounding was the movement from the countryside into the city. In 1820, about one hundred thousand people lived in cities of over ten thousand; by 1840, it was four times that. New York City alone grew from three hundred thousand to four hundred thousand in the ten years from 1830 to 1840. The rural population was increasing rapidly, too, but the urban population was growing much faster. (To learn more about the rise of cities, readers can consult *The Immigrant and the City*, the fiftheenth volume in this series.)

Thus, a new America was beginning to suggest what America would be in the future. The Jacksonian era was a time of tumult and rush, going and getting, and everywhere change.

CHAPTER IV

The Rise of the Market Economy

In the old, rural America that existed before the industrial revolution, most people did not buy things very often. There was no need to, for most people grew or made at home almost everything they needed. Wealthier families, of course, did buy furniture, books, silverware, china dishes, and much else; but these people were only a small percentage of the American population.

But with the arrival of mass-produced goods and the new transportation system to carry them cheaply around the country, things began to change. All those millions of independent farm families decided that it was more sensible to buy cheap machine-made cloth, shoes, candles, soap, and many other things, than to go through the drudgery of making them at home. Besides, the cloth coming out of the New England textile mills was smoother and more colorful than homespun; window glass let in more light than the oiled paper many farmers used in their windows; painted plates and glass mugs were handsomer and easier to clean than wooden utensils. The American appetite for buying things was whetted even more by the advertisements for products in the new, cheap newspapers.

This picture of the Talcott family, who lived in a small town in upstate New York, was painted by Deborah Goldsmith in 1832. Seventy-year-old Mary Talcott, at left, would have grown up in a house with homemade furniture and few decorations. Her son, daughter-in-law, and grandchildren have machine-made wallpaper, carpeting, furniture, and clothing, as well as large glass windows looking out on the fields outside.

We must remember that, in the 1820s, middle-class families did not have a chair for each member, nor did everyone have a separate place to sleep. Children slept two or three together, and visitors to inns commonly shared a bed with one or two others. During the Jacksonian era, not only chairs and beds but also mirrors, clocks, china cups, and a host of other household items we take for granted today, became commonplace.

By the time Andrew Jackson became president in 1829, American prosperity was rapidly increasing. Because of this prosperity, Americans were better housed, better clothed, and better fed than most people elsewhere, a situation that remains true today.

But a change in society of this magnitude was bound to bring dislocations. For one thing, it sharpened the division between the North and the South. These two sections of the country had always had their differences, as became clear during the writing of the Constitution when many of the toughest issues to settle pitted North against South. The South was committed to agriculture, particularly the growing of cotton, tobacco, rice, and a few other products. Most of the new industrial system was being built in the North, especially in New England and the Northeast generally. Increasingly, southerners became dependent on northern factories to spin their cotton, northern merchants to ship and sell their tobacco and rice, northern bankers to lend them the money they needed for seeds and farm equipment. Because North and South had different types of economies, what was good for one section was often bad for the other. For example, northern industrialists liked protective tariffs to keep down foreign competition against the clocks, cloth, glassware, axes they were making; for southerners, protective tariffs just increased the price of the goods they wanted to buy.

But the coming of industrialization to America brought more subtle and far-reaching changes, which are with us even today. Previously, independent farm families saw little actual cash through the course of the

This picture of the port of New Orleans, probably engraved in the 1850s, shows the torrent of goods, like corn and tobacco, which was flowing in from southern farms to be shipped around the world.

year and had little need for it. Now, if they wished to buy the cheap cloth, clocks, and tools coming onto the market, they had to have money. Some, especially in New England, got this money by sending family members to work in the factories springing up along rivers in the countryside. But in the time we are talking about, most farmers did not live near a factory, particularly in the South and West where there were few factories of any kind. These farmers got their cash by specializing in one type of crop, like wheat, corn, tobacco, rye, cotton. They would sell some or most of their crop and use the money to buy the other things they needed.

They were now caught up in what is called the *market economy*, tied in to a system of prices and wages. Often they ran into trouble for reasons that were out of their control. If, for example, American farmers as a whole produced more of one crop, like wheat, than there was a market for, the price of it would rapidly drop, frequently to the point where the farmers lost money on it. If there was a depression, with a lot of people out of work, there might be less demand for bread, and farmers might see a lot of their wheat rotting in their barns. In such cases farmers frequently went into debt; and when they ran into another bad spell, they might not be able to pay their loans, and the banks would foreclose on their farms.

This is precisely what happened during the nineteenth century and into the twentieth century: fewer and fewer people owned farms, and the farms became larger and larger. In 1820, some 80 percent of Americans owned farms; today it is around 1 percent. Partly this is because modern farming methods and machinery make it possible for each farmer to produce vastly more wheat, beef, corn, milk than one could have a century before. But it was also an inevitable result of the switch to the market economy in which the more successful—or luckier—farmers drove out the less successful ones.

A second group of Americans who felt drastic changes in their lives with the industrialization of America were tens of thousands of artisans and craftsmen. As we have seen, before the industrial revolution, nearly everything was made by hand one at a time. Everywhere in America, in villages, small towns, cities, there existed craftspeople specializing in making one sort of product or another: coopers who made barrels; blacksmiths who shoed horses, made nails, and other metal products; tailors who sewed shirts and dresses; wheelwrights who made wagon wheels; cobblers who made shoes. Such craftspeople sold their goods right out of their craft shops. They were usually assisted by several apprentices who lived with the master craftsman and his family, and worked for nothing more than room and board in order to learn the trade. In time they would become master craftsmen themselves.

The apprentices were treated like family members and were rewarded for good work with treats, or punished for bad behavior. The pace in the workshops was slow. Time was taken off for holidays, all hands took frequent breaks during the day for a glass of cider, a bun, and there was always a lot of gossiping and horseplay around the shop. It was not all fun and games, though: the

This illustration of a typical craftsman's shop shows two apprentices making shoes in the background, while the master measures the foot of a customer. Shoes for the wealthy were made to order, one at a time , for each patron.

work was often hard, the hours long, the masters demanding and in some cases cruel. But for many youngsters, apprenticing to a craftsman was a more desirable course than working long hours in all kinds of weather on a farm. These craft shops were not simply an economic system; they were a way of life.

With industrialization, the craft shops were rapidly pushed out of business. The factories could turn out products much more cheaply and sometimes of better quality than could the craftspeople using traditional hand methods. Soon, young apprentices who had expected to become master gunsmiths, wheelwrights, shoemakers found themselves doing routine repetitive tasks in factories for low wages. By the time of the Civil War, the village craftsman was a rarity.

In sum, during the period we are discussing, America began the momentous change from an agricultural to an industrial market economy. As should be clear, this was not merely a change of economic systems; it involved a dramatic shift in how Americans lived their lives. Increasingly, they would be coming off their one-family, independent farms to work in factories, in mines, on steamships, driving horses and wagons carrying the products spewed out by the factories. (For description of the rise of large scale industry, readers can consult the fourteenth volume in this series, *The Rise of Industry*.)

The factories, first established along country rivers, moved to towns and cities. People who had grown up in small country farm communities, where they knew everybody for miles around, now found themselves living in cramped boarding houses and often unsanitary shacks and shanties in the midst of strangers. Many of these workers were underpaid, and there was always the risk of losing your job. The immigrants flooding in from Europe, especially Germany and Ireland, were competing for the same jobs: This helped to keep wages low.

As you would expect, mill workers sometimes rebelled against their conditions. As early as 1828, when the industrial system was just getting

This drawing of a family living in a slum apartment is rather sentimentalized, but it nonetheless gives a good idea of how many, if not the majority, of big-city workers lived. Families were crowded into one or two rooms, where they often did piecework, sewing pockets onto shirts, and the like. This picture is from the 1880s, but conditions two or three decades earlier were not much different.

cranked up, workers began to join together to improve working conditions. Through the 1830s many of them formed organizations known as workingmen's parties. These were much like our modern unions, but they engaged also in political activities such as running candidates for office. Like modern unions, they sometimes went on strike. These workers' organizations put out newspapers and bulletins, which discussed many ideas for making life better for workers, such as laws limiting the workday to, say, ten hours. Some workers' groups wanted free schools for their children—in many places, especially the South, there were no public schools. They also wanted an end to debtors' prisons. Some of these ideas seemed very radical at the time; but today many of them, such as wage and hour laws, are taken for granted.

Another consequence of the industrial market economy was a growing economic inequality among the American people. Before 1820, America was a relatively egalitarian place, perhaps the most egalitarian large society there had ever been. Roughly three-quarters of Americans had about as much as everybody else. Some were prosperous, some less so; some farmers had china plates and glasses, some made do with wooden ones; some had a horse to ride to church, some walked. But the differences were not marked, and most people lived similar lives.

Blacks—mostly slaves in 1830—were nearly 16 percent of the population but did not share in this equality, nor did Indians, who, though still important in the fur trade, were not really part of the farming economy. And there were small numbers of the very rich, such as wealthy merchants in the seacoast cities and planters on huge farms, who lived in grand houses with servants, fine furniture, portraits of their wives and children on the walls. There were also small numbers of poor—floaters drifting around the big cities, working at odd jobs when they could find them, begging and stealing when they could not. On the whole, though there had been a tendency since the earliest colonial days toward a concentration of wealth in a few families, relatively speaking, wealth was fairly evenly divided in America in the nineteenth century.

That began to change with the coming of the industrial revolution and the market economy. One historian has calculated that in New York, in older times, the richest 10 percent owned almost half the wealth; by President Jackson's time, the richest 4 percent owned almost half. And by 1845, the percentage had fallen further. Another historian has figured that in 1825 in New York, Brooklyn, (then a separate city), Boston, and Philadelphia, the top 1 percent of the people owned a quarter of the wealth; by 1850, they owned half of it.

Of course—except in the plantation South—inequities of wealth were bound to be greater in the cities than in the countryside, where there were fewer wealthy people. Nonetheless, the rich in America generally were

This painting by Joseph Davis shows a typical middle-class American family in 1837 as America was starting to industrialize. Note the relatively elegant formal clothes, the matching table and chairs, the decorations. The father is reading one of the many new newspapers of the time, which carried advertisements for the stream of goods coming from the factories. Such a middle-class family was not rich but was much better off than the families of factory workers.

getting richer. But so were most people: American prosperity was rising rapidly and everybody was getting a larger slice of the pie; it was just that the wealthy people were moving ahead faster.

The industrial revolution in America took place over a long period and was not really complete until after 1900, when more workers were in mills and factories than were on farms. Slow as the change came, it was nonetheless revolutionary, for it brought with it a new class system. All societies are divided into classes, in some cases fairly loose ones, as in America today. In other cases they are clearly marked, as in medieval

The shift from the craft shops to the factories not only gave Americans access to a greater variety of goods but also changed their ways of living. At left, a craftsman builds a clock by hand, putting the machinery together and fitting it into its case, while the well-to-do customer watches. The clockmaker is supposed to be Simon Willard, one of the most famous of the early clockmakers. By contrast, in the picture below, engraved in 1851, we see clocks being mass produced by machines in a factory, while ironically a clock on the wall at rear reminds workers of how many hours they have yet to go.

Europe, where with a very few exceptions a peasant was a peasant for life, as would be his children and grandchildren.

The industrial revolution that began during the Age of Jackson created a "blue-collar" class of people who did routine tasks working with their hands in factories, in mines, on riverboats, in lumber camps. At the same time there grew up a "white-collar" class of people who worked in offices doing tasks that could also be quite routine, such as filing papers, keeping accounts, ordering supplies. But generally they were paid more and enjoyed higher status than the laborers who worked with their hands.

The class system that grew out of the burgeoning industrial system was different from the one that existed in the old rural America, when most people worked on farms or in craft shops. Americans take pride in the fact that ours is an open system, in which it is possible for anyone to rise by increasing their earnings and status—or to fall, too. And it is true that even in Andrew Jackson's time about 15 percent rose and another 15 percent fell. But then as now, most people tended to remain more or less in the kind of life they were born to.

Over the many years since Andrew Jackson's time, the whole American nation has grown, on average, more wealthy year by year, allowing for the usual ups and downs. Most of us have been moving up, and that was as true under Jackson as it is today. The average American now is wealthier in terms of his style of living than rich people were in 1840, possessed of an ease and comfort that hardly anyone had back then.

The question that remains is whether the vast wealth of America, which is by far the richest nation the world has ever seen, is entirely for the best. That question was being asked even as the new industrial system, with the market economy, was rising in the land. Americans, many philosophers said, were becoming too "materialistic," too concerned with acquiring possessions at the expense of other values. Perhaps, the philosophers said, people would be happier if they put less emphasis on things, and more on religion and their relationships with their friends, family, neighbors, and community. Would it not make for a richer life to get together with other people to help raise a barn, husk the corn crop, make a quilt, play a game, or just to talk, rather than spending the time worrying about getting a gold ring or fancy new clothes?

One philosopher of those days, Ralph Waldo Emerson, said, "Things are in the saddle and ride mankind." In Emerson's opinion, Americans had enslaved themselves with their driving desire for the newest gadget, the most recent fashion. The famous French observer Alexis de Tocqueville, who, in the 1830s, studied the new United States carefully, said, "I know of no country, indeed, where the love of money has taken stronger hold on the affections of men." And Washington Irving, one of America's first great popular writers, coined the term "the almighty dollar," which he said was "that great object of universal devotion throughout the land." The dollar, according to Irving, was an American god.

For many Americans, already middle-aged when the market revolution took hold, the new culture of materialism and upward striving was hard to get accustomed to. Often they had been brought up with the old Puritan values of thrift, moderation, hard work, and self-denial. All this striving toward a life full of luxuries made them uncomfortable and anxious. There were fewer satisfactions from buying things, they felt, than from making them yourself; and more satisfaction in a quiet churchly Sunday with your family than in owning a new mirror or beaver hat.

Few people deny that material prosperity is a good thing: surely it is better to have plenty of food and clothing than to do without. The question is, what does it cost? It is a point which has been much debated in America since the time of Jackson.

CHAPTER V

The Beginnings of the Two-Party Political System

Andrew Jackson was involved in two developments which continue to have a great significance for Americans today. One was the creation of what has been called the "modern president." We shall see what we mean by that in the next chapter. The other was the rise of the two-party system. We will look at that first.

The Constitution of the United States says nothing whatever about political parties. In fact, the Founding Fathers hated the hole idea of parties. They had seen, in England, the Whig and Tory parties constantly at each other's throats. Washington, Madison, and the others firmly believed that members of parties almost always put the needs of their parties ahead of the welfare of their nation. That is, they were more concerned with getting into office and staying in when they got there than with following the best policies for their country. Furthermore, party members expected to get good government jobs when their side took over; often, corrupt and incompetent politicians ended up holding important positions. For these reasons, the men who wrote the Constitution forty years before Jackson became president made no provision for political parties and sincerely hoped that there wouldn't be any.

But when we look back on it, we can see that parties were almost inevitable. In Washington's first government, his secretary of state, Thomas Jefferson, and his secretary of the treasury, Alexander Hamilton, had opposite opinions on many important subjects. People who took one side or the other began to work together with Hamilton or Jefferson to push the government their way. These two groups were not political parties as we use the term today: they did not hold conventions, did not write out policy platforms, did not fly campaign banners. They were more like factions, or interest groups, as we might say today. Nonetheless, they were semiorganized factions, and they came to have names, the Federalists and the Republicans. (The Republicans had nothing to do with the modern Republican Party. Readers interested in more detail on the Federalists and Republicans can consult the seventh volume in this series, called *Building A New Nation*.)

The Federalists held power until 1800, when they were decisively beaten by the Republicans. The Federalists never again gained the presidency, although they continued to have strength in Congress and in some states. By 1816, with the election of the Republican candidate James Monroe, the Federalists had just about withered away. It seemed to some people that the "party spirit" was dying out, and they began speaking of the time as an "era of good feeling." Only the Republicans were left, and in 1820, James Monroe ran without any opposition, the only time after Washington's two elections that has ever happened in the United States.

Nonetheless, whatever was said about an era of good feeling, there were bobbing around in the American political sea several groups and factions with their own ideas, eager for power. These were still not political parties, but they were the material out of which parties would be formed.

Of particular importance to their formation was that the rules of the

In 1820, James Monroe was elected to the presidency unopposed, the only time—since George Washington's two elections—that has ever happened in the United States. Many people believed that the "spirit of party" was over and an era of good feeling was beginning. In fact, by the next election the spirit of party was stronger than ever.

game had been changed. As we have seen, in George Washington's day America was a deferential society, in which some would lead and some would follow. Rules for voting had been set up so that only property-owning white males actually got to vote. In any event, state legislatures, not the voters, chose presidential electors in most cases. A relatively small number of men could decide many elections.

But as the deferential attitudes were pushed aside after 1800 by the new idea that each person was as good as the next, the voting rules were changed to suit. As one historian has said, between 1800 and 1840 there was a "hidden revolution" in America. By 1832, most of the states were choosing presidential electors by popular vote. By 1842, all states were divided up into Congressional districts instead of holding statewide elections; this made it easier for voters to hear their Congressional candidates speak, even to know them personally. It also allowed minorities, like the Germans clustered in certain parts of Pennsylvania, to elect one of their own to Congress.

The number of people who could now vote had multiplied. This meant that candidates could no longer get elected to office by gaining the support of a few key leaders. They had to appeal to a lot of people of diverse backgrounds, concerns, and wealth. The modern style of campaigning, with slogans, newspaper advertisements, fiery speeches, was on the way.

Aiding the formation of a new system was the fact that the new voting rules gave all states roughly similar election systems. This made it easier for parties to organize state groups in the same way.

As we have seen, nobody ran against James Monroe in 1820. Nonetheless, there were still all those factions bobbing around, and, in 1824, many candidates put themselves forward, among them John C. Calhoun, a much-admired politician from South Carolina; the celebrated war hero Andrew Jackson from Tennessee; Henry Clay, a Kentuckian who was a leading man in Congress; John Quincy Adams, diplomat, secretary of state, and son of the second president, John Adams. These men were nominated, not by any party, but by state legislatures. A small group of Republican congressmen nominated another candidate, William Crawford.

We must realize that in those days politicians were held in great esteem by Americans. At the time, there was little professional entertainment—few traveling shows, and of course no movies or television. People liked to hear long, dramatic or emotional speeches and came in mobs to listen to candidates make their orations. Calhoun, Clay, and others like Daniel Webster were vastly admired for their ability to make speeches that captivated audiences for hours. Orations of this kind were a major part of the new style of politics.

With so many candidates, the 1824 election was going to be close. Calhoun decided he could not win and dropped out in order to run for vice president. Jackson won the largest number of popular and electoral votes, but he did not have a majority of either. Under our constitutional system, the choice was thrown into the House of Representatives, where the choice must be made from among the top three electoral vote getters. Clay came in fourth, and he asked his supporters to vote for Adams, who won. It was said later that Clay had made "a corrupt bargain" with Adams to be named secretary of state, and, in fact, Adams did appoint Clay to that office. But historians have found no evidence that a deal was made.

The contest left a good deal of bitterness in some of the losers, and in the months that followed, the Republicans split into two factions: The National Republicans, led by John Quincy Adams and Henry Clay; and the Democratic Republicans, led by Andrew Jackson. Calhoun, despite the fact that he had been elected vice president with Adams, decided to side with Jackson's Democratic Republicans.

This split foreshadowed our party system. As early as 1825, when the next election was three years away, Andrew Jackson resigned from the Senate and began to put together a campaign machine that was much like the ones that candidates build today. In this he was very much aided by one of the

The election of 1824 was very bitterly contested. John Quincy Adams, the only son of a president to become president himself, won, but the election left the old Republican party split into two factions.

new technologies arising at that time—the transportation system based on steamboats and canals. Jackson traveled around the country meeting newspaper editors, politicians, and voters. Newspapers, in particular, spread Jackson's word. Soon his party, the Democratic Republicans, shortened its name to the Democrats. Thus was founded the present-day Democratic Party, the oldest political party in the world.

A key figure in the formation of political parties was Martin Van Buren, an astute politician from New York State. Van Buren was a great organizer. He put together a group of powerful men in his state to support Andrew Jackson in the 1824 elections. Although Jackson lost to John Quincy Adams, Van Buren felt that he would win the next time, and he started to build the Democrats in his state into a modern type of political party, with branches in every town and county in New York. Basic to Van Buren's system was "patronage," in which the party in power would give out government jobs to people who had been helpful to it, thus assuring their loyalty. Van Buren and his associates saw nothing wrong with this. They believed that they had a duty to protect the people against the rich and powerful who ran banks, investment houses, businesses. In order for the people to prevail, they had to be part of a strong party controlled from the top. The New York Democrats under Van Buren became nationally powerful and formed the model for political organizations elsewhere. One historian has said that Van Buren "may be considered the principal architect of the modern American political party."

In 1828, the group of Republicans remaining after the Jackson Democrats split off nominated John Quincy Adams for a second term. Jackson, however, campaigned as both a celebrated war hero and a representative of the common man. His battles against the Indians gave him support in states like Alabama and Georgia where large tribes clung to rich farm lands desired by whites. Jackson's base in the West made him popular in Tennessee, Kentucky, and Ohio. His running mate, Calhoun, brought him support elsewhere in the South and middle states, and Van Buren's organization helped him in the Northeast. Jackson's popularity and organization proved too much for Adams to overcome. Jackson won convincingly, and Adams, like his father, became a one-term president.

In the next elections—in 1832—all parties held conventions in which to nominate candidates, and one of them, a short-lived third party, put forth a party policy platform. The National Republicans nominated one of its stars, Henry Clay, and the Democrats, of course, nominated Jackson again. Jackson won in a landslide with Martin Van Buren as his vice president.

Two years later, John Calhoun brought his supporters into what was left of the old Republican party. This party was a kind of grab bag of politicians who were united mostly in their opposition to Andrew Jackson. It included some of the most celebrated men

In 1840, the Whigs were still calling themselves the Democratic Whigs, as this drawing of a campaign headquarters shows.

of the times, among them Clay, Adams, Calhoun, and Daniel Webster. They decided to call themselves Whigs, after the British political party sympathetic to Americans during the Revolution. Now there was a true two-party system in America, with most of the important statesmen and politicians belonging to one or the other. In 1836, Jackson followed the tradition set by Washington when he retired after two terms. The Democrats nominated Jackson's vice president, the shrewd Martin Van Buren. The Whigs did not hold a convention but nominated several people who were popular in their own states, in hopes that nobody would get a majority, and the House of Representatives would have to decide as it had in 1824. The popularity of Jackson made the Democrats the stronger party, at least for the moment, and Van Buren won a clear majority.

By the next election, in 1840, the two-party system was firmly established. Both Whigs and Democrats held conventions. The Democrats nominated Van Buren again. Many Whigs wished to nominate their best politician, the astute Henry Clay, but they feared that some of his policies would be unpopular with voters. Instead they nominated an old hero of the Indian wars, William Henry Harrison, who had won an important battle against the Indians on the Tippecanoe River in Indiana. Harrison had no known policies to make him unpopular, and the Whigs based their campaign on personalities, rather than ideas, as many presidential campaigns have since done.

Fortunately for them, a Democratic newspaper said scornfully that if Harrison were given a small pension, he would happily retire to his "log cabin" with a "barrel of cider." The newspaper's point was that Harrison was an ignoramus, unfit to be president. The Whigs turned the idea on its head and presented Harrison in their advertisements and rallies as a plain man of the people. In fact Harrison, a general, came from an aristocratic Virginia family and lived in a grand mansion on the banks of the Ohio River.

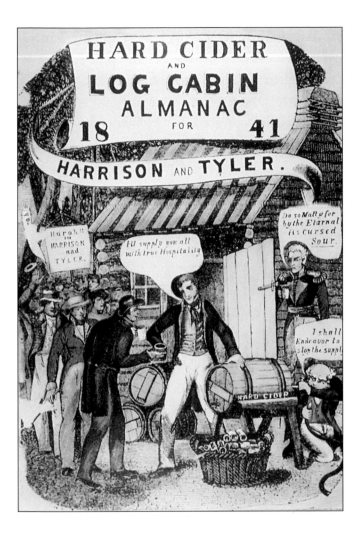

"The log cabin and cider" campaign in support of William Henry Harrison made it appear that Harrison was "a man of the people," as Andrew Jackson actually was. Jackson had grown up in a cabin and preferred homely hard cider to fancy wines.

The Whigs cooked up a slogan, "Tippecanoe and Tyler, too," referring to the vice presidential candidate, John Tyler. They had a song written which included their slogan and mentioned cider. At their rallies, they sometimes built log cabins, which they filled with barrels of hard cider—apple wine, really, the drink of the common man—to hand out to voters.

Harrison beat Van Buren decisively. In large measure that was because of a depression, which the voters blamed on Van Buren. But no doubt the famous "log cabin and cider" campaign tactics helped to give

Harrison support, and it started the long-standing tradition of the modern presidential campaign, with its posters, buttons, campaign songs, and large rallies. Ironically, Harrison died after only a month in office, and his vice president, John Tyler, took over, the first vice president to succeed to the presidency, and often called by his opponents, "His Accidency."

In fact, as this picture suggests, William Henry Harrison was a general and an aristocrat who lived in a large mansion. It was hardly the first time that a candidate for office made himself appear to be something other than what he was.

CHAPTER VI

Andrew Jackson and the Modern Presidency

Although Martin Van Buren has been seen as the chief architect of the modern political party, Andrew Jackson also played an important role in creating the national Democratic Party. He was not the careful organizer that Van Buren was, but he was a very shrewd politician with an astute sense of public opinion, who could make friends with people and get them on his side. As a war hero, he was much admired, and he knew how to use his celebrity to his advantage. He and Van Buren thus made a team—Jackson out front, attracting voters with his fame and down-home manner; Van Buren behind the scenes, building a solid organization.

Jackson's role in creating a presidential style which many presidents follow today was even clearer. Once again we have to look back at the Constitution. The Founding Fathers created a system of "checks and balances" by which three arms of government, the President, the Congress, and the Supreme Court, would check each other from taking too much power. But in fact the framers of the Constitution assumed that the Congress would play the most active role in setting policy and writing laws for Americans.

Andrew Jackson had a somewhat different opinion. He was a very strong-willed man who had great faith in his own judgments. In his view, the president was elected by *all* the people, not just some of them as each congressman was. Therefore, according to Jackson, the president's views ought to carry special weight. He frequently lectured Congress on its duties, and he did not much like compromising with it and fought fiercely for policies he wanted.

Surprisingly, although Jackson believed in a strong *president*, he did not believe in strong *government*. He felt that government ought not to meddle in the citizens' affairs too much but should let Americans go on about their business. The main job of a president was to prevent people in places of power, like bankers, wealthy businessmen, government officials, from exploiting the government to get special privileges for themselves. Jackson believed that it took a strong president to do that.

We can best understand Jackson's philosophy by looking at two of his hardest political fights as president. One involved the national bank. The idea of a national bank had always been controversial. Some people even believed that, as the Constitution said nothing about a national bank, such a thing was unconstitutional. But others believed that a national bank was necessary to the smooth running of the banking system and the economy in general. (For an explanation of how the Bank of the United States came to be, see the volume in this series called *Building a New Nation*.)

The details of the squabble over the national bank are a bit complicated. We need only to know that Jackson believed that the bank's policies hurt small farmers and working people in order to benefit businessmen. The head of the national bank, Nicholas Biddle, was as strong-willed as Jackson, and even more arrogant, and would not take advice from anyone. Historians today say that in fact, much of what Biddle did was sensible. But it is also true that during a depression that began in 1819, the national bank forced the foreclosure of a lot of mortgages, so

This caricature, drawn in 1837 when many people were suffering from hard times, shows a woman and a child begging (center), men out of work (right), a drunken family ignoring their child (left), and people flooding into a pawnshop (left rear). The problem is suggested by signs on the buildings at rear: the custom house will accept only specie—that is, hard money—while the bank next door displays a sign saying "No specie payments made here." Everybody wanted to give paper money for the things they bought but always wanted to get specie for the things they sold.

that thousands of people lost their farms and their homes. One commentator said, "The Bank was saved, and the people were ruined."

By the time Jackson became president, he was firmly against the bank. This was in part because, while the bank gave loans to many anti-Jackson congressmen, it refused to give them to Jackson's supporters—thus, in Jackson's mind, corrupting Congress. But for the most part, Jackson's opposition to the bank had to do with the issue of paper money. It will surprise modern readers to learn at that time there was no official paper money—the dollar bills, fives, and tens we are so familiar with. The United States government issued only gold and silver coins. But it was obviously inconvenient, and sometimes almost impossible, to cart around the huge amounts of coins needed to make a large purchase—for example, a merchant buying a new ship.

Thus, people used notes issued by private banks, insurance companies, and other corporations for paper money. These notes could in theory be exchanged at the bank for gold and silver coins if anyone wanted to. In practice, however, far more paper money was issued than there was gold and silver to back it up. People were always a little suspicious of paper money and did not value it as highly as what they thought of as "real" money in gold and silver. The result was that a shopkeeper might consider a ten-dollar note to be worth only, say, eight dollars and would give only eight dollars worth of goods for it. There were about seven thousand banks and other corporations issuing these notes. Thus, it was impossible for any but the most active merchant to know what they were worth at any given moment. As a consequence, workers whose wages were paid in these bank notes and farmers who got them in exchange for produce were often knowingly cheated by the more sophisticated businessmen they dealt with. A lot of people, then, wanted a "hard money" system.

Jackson agreed. He believed that having paper notes issued by state banks was unconstitutional. (The term state bank refers to banks whose corporate charters were granted by state governments. Biddle's Bank of the United States was the only one chartered by the U.S. government.) Jackson kept trying to curb the powers of Biddle's national bank, but Nicholas Biddle was determined to run the bank as he wanted and refused to compromise with Jackson. When the bank's charter was renewed by Congress, Jackson vetoed it. But the old charter would not run out until 1836. Then, in the election of 1832, the Whigs decided to use Jackson's veto of the law chartering the bank as an issue against him. Jackson was enraged. "The bank is trying to kill me," he shouted, "but I will kill it."

And he did. As required by the law, the government had deposited its money in Biddle's national bank. Jackson told his secretary of the treasury to take the government's money out of the national bank. This would set up a chain reaction: in order to have enough money in his bank to keep going, Biddle would have to call in loans he had made to businessmen around the country. These businessman would then have to call in the loans and mortgages they had made to people in their localities. A side effect of this general calling in of notes and loans would be the disappearance of a good deal of paper money, which was all to the good as far as Jackson was concerned.

However, Jackson's secretary of the treasury refused to take the government's money out of the national bank, because it was against the law. Jackson transferred him to another job. His successor also refused to withdraw the government's money, and Jackson fired him. Finally Jackson got a secretary of the treasury who would withdraw the money. The chain reaction occurred, and a number of local banks shut down because they couldn't collect a lot of their loans and as a consequence did not have enough money to pay their loans to Biddle's national bank. Finally, the national bank had to shut down, too. Jackson had won, but he had had to ride roughshod over Congress and the law to do it. His veto of the bank charter was perfectly legal, but the senate censured Jackson for his actions. Ironically, the chain reaction triggered an economic depression, with banks failing, farms being foreclosed, and people being thrown out of work. This depression was a major factor in the defeat of Jackson's ally, Martin Van Buren, when he ran for a second term against "Tippecanoe" Harrison in 1840.

This cartoon shows Andrew Jackson, seated with pipe, exulting in his victory over Nicholas Biddle and the National Bank.

Jackson, thus, was willing to use dubious tactics to get what he wanted. He felt comfortable doing so, for he always believed that he was acting in the best interests of the people. In another major battle of his presidency, which historians call the *nullification crisis*, he showed great strength and determination, as well as the tendency to get tough with people who opposed him.

As we have seen, southerners were generally opposed to protective tariffs—taxes on imports—because they just made the things they bought more expensive. Ironically, one of the major figures in creating the protective tariffs was the South Carolinian John Calhoun. The South,

Calhoun saw, had plenty of rivers for water power and an almost endless supply of cotton at hand; surely it would build its own mills. But southerners found it easier and more profitable in the short run to go on growing cotton with black slaves than to start factories. So profits from the booming textile industry continued to go to the North.

South Carolina in particular suffered economically from this and other causes. South Carolinians were bitter, and the protective tariff became for them an emotional issue. They felt that they were being exploited generally by the North. Calhoun himself began to change his mind about the virtues of the protective tariff.

But despite the feelings in the South, in 1828 the people in favor of the tariff had enough power in Congress to shove through an increase. Southern resentment against both the federal government and the North waxed fiercely. Behind a good deal of this resentment lay something else: southern fear that northern congressmen wanted to pass laws against slavery. A number of vocal northerners felt strongly that slavery was wrong, and a movement to abolish it was growing. If the federal govern-

Another cartoon shows a starving southerner, burdened by tariffs and taxes, joined in union to a robust northerner whose manufacturing business is supported by protective tariffs. The issue was a hot one with southerners.

ment could shove a protective tariff down southern throats, might it not also interfere with slavery? This fear was particularly strong in South Carolina, where black slaves actually outnumbered whites. If the slaves were freed and made citizens, they could outvote whites and elect a black governor and a black legislature. Though virtually no one in the 1820s was suggesting giving the vote to African-Americans, white South Carolinians were horrified by such an idea.

For the South, the answer to the problem lay in a theory worked out by the brilliant John Calhoun, who, ironically, was at the moment Jackson's vice president. Calhoun and Jackson disagreed on many points,

This sketch, by an amateur artist, Lewis Miller, who drew pictures of daily life in Virginia, shows a group of blacks being marched into Tennessee from Virginia. Blacks outnumbered whites in many places, and white southerners were fearful that the federal government would attempt to give them their freedom.

and Calhoun had no problem taking issue with the president. His theory of nullification went like this: the United States was a compact among *sovereign* states. (Sovereign means having complete power, that there is no higher power.) Thus, the people in each state had the right to nullify any federal law that appeared to go beyond the powers given to Congress by the Constitution. Congress could then either withdraw the law in question, or it could propose a constitutional amendment to make it legal. If the amendment went through, the state could either accept the new law or withdraw from the Union.

The idea of nullification had been proposed before, although not in this complete form. When it was brought up in the Senate, Daniel Webster immediately responded. He said that the American union was not a compact of sovereign states but was the creation of the people: "It is the people's constitution, the people's government, made for the people, made by the people, and answerable to the people." This, too, was

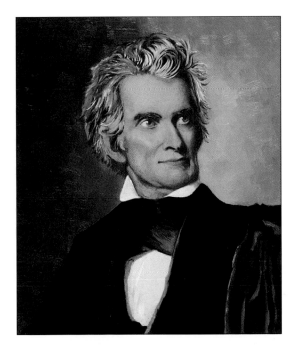

not a new idea, but had been brought up at the Constitutional Convention. Virtually all historians believe that events since Calhoun's time have borne out Webster's argument. But before the Civil War in the 1860s, the issue

Southern statesman John Calhoun worked up an ingenious "nullification" theory, by which states could reject federal laws they did not like. Most historians believe Calhoun's theory does not hold up.

was not clear. Many political and judicial leaders considered the United States a federation of at least semisovereign states.

Webster's speech was not just a well-reasoned legal argument against nullification. It was also a strongly emotional call for the preservation of the Union at all costs. He cried out to all Americans to support that "sentiment, dear to every true American heart—Liberty *and* Union, now and forever, one and inseparable." Webster's speech is one of the most famous ever given in Congress and for generations was memorized by school children and recited in classrooms. It helped to make the idea of preserving the Union an emotional matter for millions of Americans.

Jackson, so far as we know, was not a particularly strong supporter of protective tariffs, if indeed he favored them at all. But he was strongly for the preservation of the Union and, characteristically, was not going to tolerate any defiance of the government's authority. In opposing Calhoun, he repeated Webster's argument and went on to say that the Union was forever and that no state could leave. He then got Congress to pass a "force bill," which reaffirmed the government's right to use the army and navy to put down any resistance to federal authority.

But Jackson was a good politician, so he offered to reduce some of the tariffs the South so heatedly objected to. With this move a lot of the wind went out of the nullification sails. Many southerners felt that if they could get the tariffs reduced, why fight on for a theory? Meanwhile, Henry Clay, Jackson's old political opponent who was now a dominant figure in Congress, negotiated a compromise with Calhoun on the tariffs. It was Clay's compromise, but once again Jackson had won.

Southerners, however, believed that they had won, for as they saw it, through a show of strength they had gotten the hated protective tariff substantially modified. Most critically, the nullification crisis had turned what was really an economic dispute into a highly emotional issue for both North and South. Further divisions over other matters during the course of the next thirty years would lead to the Civil War.

A more compromising president than Andrew Jackson might not have forced the nullification issue out into the open in its plainest terms. A wiser one might have seen how the nation was splitting and tried to calm the passions of both North and South in order to bind up the wounds. But a man with a fighting temperament like Jackson was not likely to look for peaceful solutions when faced with a direct challenge to his authority.

Thus, we can see that while a lot of developments, like the technology and the new forward-looking spirit, substantially affected the Age of Jackson, it is also true that the character of the president had its effects. For example, before Jackson, presidents followed the line that Congress was the basic arm of government, with the president there to check its excesses; all previous presidents together had vetoed only nine acts of Congress, and then usually only because they thought the acts unconstitutional. Jackson, however, vetoed twelve bills, sometimes for unconstitutionality but often simply because he disagreed with them. Jackson believed that the Congress was likely to be driven hither and thither by sectional winds from the North, South, and West. He believed it was up to the president to set the direction for the nation and keep it firmly on course. Most presidents since have tried to do the same.

CHAPTER VII

Pushing the Indians Back Again

The attitude of whites toward the Indians around them in America was confused and contradictory, to say the least. Right from the time of the first settlements in Jamestown and Plymouth, newly arriving people, mostly English, were not sure what they ought to do about the Indians. The Indians, of course, had been on the land for thousands of years. On the other hand, Europe was suffering from unemployment and other problems; it seemed to Europeans that there was plenty of spare land in America and that they therefore had a right to take some of it over. (For the story of European-Indian relations in the colonial era, see the volume in this series called *The Clash of Cultures*.)

Many of the whites believed that the European culture, with its technology, written language, and Christian religion, was so clearly superior to the Indian cultures that the Indians would be happy to Europeanize themselves. As early nineteenth-century Americans saw it, the Indians could become integrated into white society, build themselves farmhouses like those of the whites, learn to read and write, and adopt Christianity. And some did. But most Indians, like people everywhere, were determined to hang onto the ways and religions they were raised with. Instead of mingling with whites, they wanted to go on living in their own villages, doing things the way their ancestors had done them, though with the addition of nontraditional goods like guns, plows, wagons, and unfortunately, liquor.

But the pressure on them from whites was intense. The exploding white population always wanted more land. It was very difficult for the federal government to stop people from crossing over into Indian territory on the frontier and making their own deals with the Indians, even though it was against the law. Many of these deals were fraudulent. In other cases, settlers simply took over the land and began clearing it. It is also true that Indians at times sold land that was not theirs to sell.

Right from the beginning, the Indians, too, had followed contradictory policies toward the incoming whites. Sometimes they made alliances with whites for purposes of their own; sometimes they fought them.

By the time of Andrew Jackson's presidency, the scattered farmers and the Indians on the frontier were living in constant tension, with actual fighting breaking out frequently. Frontier families lived in fear of sudden Indian raids; Indians had always to be on guard against retaliatory attacks by whites. By 1820, many whites, especially frontier setters, believed that the only good Indian was a dead Indian. Many Indians, in turn, felt that they could save their lands only by driving out the whites with all-out war.

The Indians at times were able to beat the whites in battle. In the years before 1812, a great chief, Tecumseh, tried to unify all the Indian tribes along the frontier, from Canada down to the Gulf of Mexico. He had some success, but in the end the American army was too powerful for him, and by 1820 most of the Indians in the northern areas had been driven across the Mississippi. A major Indian effort in 1832 to drive white settlers back, the Black Hawk War, also failed.

In the southern areas of the frontier, there remained a large number of Indians, especially in Mississippi, Alabama, and western portions of

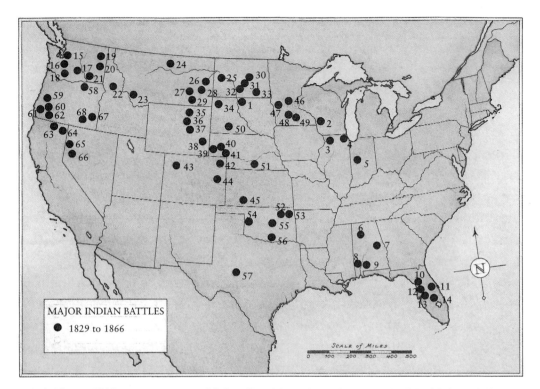

MAJOR INDIAN BATTLES
● 1829 to 1866

SCALE of MILES
0   100   200   300   400   500

1. Arickaro - 1829	24. Bear Paw Mountains - 1877	47. Wood Lake - 1862
2. Bad Ax - 1832	25. Kill Deer Mountain - 1864	48. Red Wood Ferry - 1862
3. Stillman's Defeat - 1832	26. Cedar Creek - 1876	49. New Ulm - 1862
4. Fort Dearborn - 1812	27. Yellow Stone - 1879	50. Wounded Knee - 1890
5. Tippecanoe - 1811	28. Little Big Horn - 1876	51. Fort Kearney - 1867
6. Talladega - 1813	29. Roesbud - 1876	52. Round Mountain - 1861
7. Horseshoe Bend - 1814	30. Stony Lake - 1863	53. Chastenahloh - 1861
8. Fort Mims - 1813	31. Dead Buffalo Lake - 1863	54. Washita - 1868
9. Burnt Corn - 1813	32. Big Mound - 1863	55. Bird Creek - 1861
10. Withladoochee - 1835	33. White Stone Hill - 1863	56. Wichita Village - 1858
11. Fort Mellon - 1837	34. Slim Buttes - 1876	57. Dove Creek - 1863
12. Wahoo Swamp - 1835	35. Fetterman's Defeat - 1868	58. Umatilla - 1848
13. Dade Massacre - 1835	36. Hole-in-the-Wall - 1876	59. Grove Creek - 1855
14. Lake Okeechobee - 1837	37. Point of Rocks - 1874	60. Evens Creek - 1853
15. Seattle - 1856	38. Grottan's Defeat - 1854	61. The Meadows - 1856
16. Connell's Prairie - 1856	39. Mud Springs - 1865	62. Rome River - 1851
17. Haller's Defeat - 1855	40. Rush Creek - 1865	63. Lara Beds - 1873
18. Cascades - 1856	41. Ash Hollow - 1855	64. Pit River - 1867
19. Four Lakes - 1858	42. Fort Sedgwick - 1865	65. Pyramid Lake - 1860
20. Steptoe Butte - 1858	43. Milk Creek - 1879	66. Truckee - 1860
21. Walla-Walla - 1855	44. Sandcreek - 1859	67. Owyhee Forks - 1866
22. Clearwater - 1855	45. Crooked Creek - 1859	68. Lake Abert - 1866
23. Big Hole - 1877	46. Acton - 1862	

North Carolina and Georgia. Four strong tribes dominated this area of southeastern United States: The Chickasaw, the Choctaw, the Cherokee, and the Creek. In Florida there was another strong tribe, the Seminoles.

These tribes had long histories in this land—though some tribes had come into the area only one or two hundred years before the whites. They had rich cultures, and remained strong. They had been lucky, for whites had been slower to move into the area than they had done elsewhere in the nation. But by the 1820s, with the invention of the cotton gin in 1793 followed by the rapid development of the New England textile industry, there were fortunes to be made in growing cotton. The Cotton Kingdom was spreading, and the vast fertile lands held by the southeastern Indians were smack in the middle of the best cotton-growing land in the country. It was thus not just homesteaders who were eyeing this sun-drenched land, but also wealthy cotton growers and speculators. The governments of the states involved often included the very planters and speculators who were covetously eyeing the Indians' land, and they were not much interested in the Indians' rights in the matter.

Andrew Jackson had ambiguous feelings about the Indians. On the one hand, as a frontier soldier he had fought both with and against Indians. He knew them and their culture better than most Americans did, and he respected them. On the other hand, he was driven by a desire to see white America rise into greatness, and he felt that the Indians could not be allowed to stand in the way.

A second consideration in Jackson's mind was that various Indian groups, for a couple of centuries, had from time to time made alliances with enemies of America, especially the British, French, and Spanish, in order to halt the westward flow of Americans. They might do so again, and it appeared to Jackson that the Indians were a back door through which foreign enemies might enter.

Finally, Jackson was philosophically inclined to let states run their own affairs, so long as they did not try to challenge federal authority as they had during the nullification crisis. Unfortunately for the Indians, the governments of the southeastern states were quite prepared to aid the planters and speculators in running the Indians out, though constitutionally only the federal government could make treaties with Indians.

Jackson did have some sympathy for the Indians, but not enough to stop the states from doing what they wanted about them. In the end he concluded that the only solution was to remove the Indians to new lands across the Mississippi. Removal would solve in a stroke many of the whites' problems with the Indians. And while it was likely that whites would eventually push across the Mississippi, as small numbers were already doing, the land there was huge, and Indians settled in it, most

The Indians were constantly being pushed farther and farther west as settlers flooded over the Allegheny Mountains, thence to the Mississippi, and finally across the Mississippi into the Louisiana Territory. The advance guard moving into the new territory were the "mountain men," who went out after beaver and other skins and proved invaluable in guiding settlers through the rough territory. One of the most famous of the mountain men was Joseph Reddeford Walker, shown here in a sketch by Alfred Jacob Miller, who visited the territory in 1837 and knew Walker well.

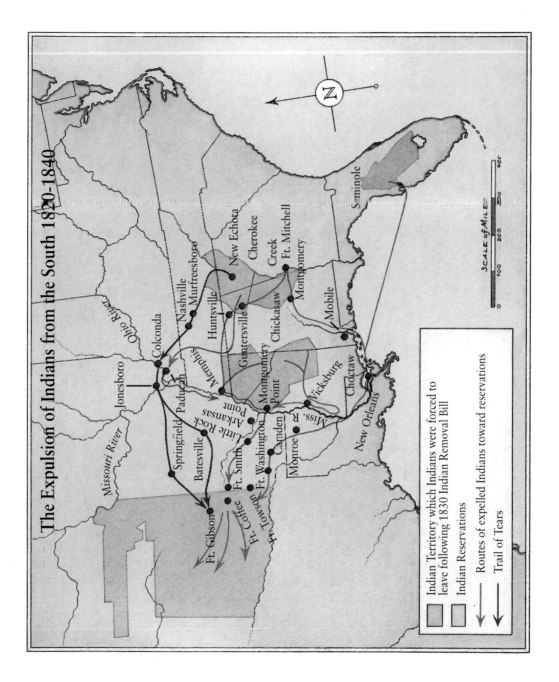

The Expulsion of Indians from the South 1820-1840

Indian Territory which Indians were forced to leave following 1830 Indian Removal Bill

Indian Reservations

→ Routes of expelled Indians toward reservations

→ Trail of Tears

people believed, would not be threatened for many decades to come. (Few people had any idea how rapidly the West would be settled.) As a matter of practical fact, Jackson believed, removal was the only way the Indians could keep their tribes and their cultures intact. If they stayed, they would be destroyed.

Jackson, however, did not want to run the Indians out by force if he could avoid it. If they agreed to leave peaceably, the federal government would provide them with ample new lands, help in traveling to them, and a good deal of money as well. This began one of the saddest tales in the long history of relations between whites and Indians, the story of the Trail of Tears.

Andrew Jackson was not the first president to call for the removal of Indians. Thomas Jefferson a generation earlier had come to believe that the only way their culture could be saved was to move the Indians to new lands to the west, where they would be safe from whites for generations. Other presidents carried on this policy, and certain Indian groups were moved westward, especially from Ohio, Illinois, and nearby areas. But many people had felt that this policy was unfair to the Indians, and it had not been pushed hard.

Andrew Jackson, as ever, was sure that his policy was for the best and was prepared to press it aggressively. At the beginning of his administration in 1829, he asked Congress to authorize his removal policy. He was astonished by the uproar that followed. Newspapers, ordinary citizens, and many important congressmen insisted that removal was grossly unfair. It went against numerous treaties and promises the United States government had made. Senator Frederick Theodore Frelinghuysen of New Jersey made a long, impassioned speech in support of Indian rights, during which he said: "We have crowded the tribes upon a few miserable acres of our Southern frontier: it is all that is left to them of their once boundless forests: and still, like the horse-leech, our insatiable cupidity cries give! give! give!"

Whites were constantly changing the terms of treaties they made with Indians. In this negotiation, representatives of several plains Indian tribes, including Sioux and Sacs and Foxes, met with Lewis Cass of Michigan and William Clark of Missouri, at Prarie du Chien to sign the Great Treaty. Clark had been one of the leaders of the celebrated Lewis and Clark expedition which crossed the plains and the Rockies. The presence of American soldiers made it quite clear to the Indians that they would have to give in to American demands.

Many other congressmen supported Indian rights. So strong was the feeling against removal that the vote in the House of Representatives was very close, 102 to 97. It passed only because Jackson himself personally pressed many congressmen to vote for removal.

The main targets of the Indian removal policy were the five large and prosperous tribes of the Southeast: 20,000 Cherokee, 22,000 Choctaw, 4,000 Seminole, 22,000 Creek, and 5,000 Chickasaw—over 70,000 people altogether. All of them had been harassed for several years by whites, with both official and unofficial support from the state governments. For example, in the 1820s the Mississippi government began insisting that the Choctaw were not an independent nation, but merely citizens of Mississippi; the legislature therefore felt justified in passing laws abolishing tribal governments and in threatening to jail chiefs who tried to govern in traditional ways. The tribal leaders pointed out to the government in Washington that treaties gave them the right to run their own affairs as they had always done. The federal government only replied that it was helpless to prevent the states from doing what they wanted to do. White settlers squatted on Indian land and stole Indian livestock. The Indians could do nothing in response, for they knew that white law officers would not protect them. The Creeks, similarly, had their tribal rights taken away from them by the Mississippi government.

The Cherokee had an additional problem. In 1829, gold was discovered in the mountains of northern Georgia, on Cherokee land. The

Left, Tsholocha, a Cherokee, and right, Tulope, a Choctaw, painted by Karl Bodmer at the time that Andrew Jackson was putting through his Indian removal program. Note that the Indians are wearing clothing that combine features of white and Indian costume.

Georgia legislature forbade the Cherokee from mining gold on their own land. White prospectors stampeded over the gold fields, pulling down fences, stealing household goods, and creating chaos. The Indians went to court, where they were told that they could not testify against whites.

What is sadly ironic about the attacks on the southeastern Indians is that they, more than any other Indian groups of the time, were doing just what the whites had always said they wanted Indians to do—become Europeanized. Many of them had built farmhouses and were raising corn and hogs, wearing European-style clothes, and going to Christian churches. The Cherokee in particular had taken up white ways. One white who visited the Cherokee nation said, "We saw several houses built of hewn stone, superior to any we had ever seen before. The people seemed to have more money than the whites in our own settlements; they were better clothed. The women were weaving, the men cultivating corn, and raising beef and pork in abundance."

Hundreds of Choctaws engaging in a type of ball game, painted by George Catlin, who was famous for painting Indians, after their removal across the Mississippi to new lands. Note the tall goalposts at left and right.

Two principal Cherokee leaders had been trained for the ministry in Connecticut and had married white women they met there. Religious missionaries were running schools for Cherokee children. Sequoya, who has been termed a "Cherokee genius," worked out an alphabet for the Cherokee language, and a Cherokee was publishing a tribal newspaper written in both English and Cherokee languages. The Cherokee even drew up a constitution and formed a republic.

At first these southeastern tribes resisted the removal policy. The Cherokee, who were literate and understood a good deal about law and the Constitution, decided in 1831 to go to court to gain their rights. Among other things, Georgia had claimed that it was not bound by the federal treaties with the Indians. The Cherokees insisted that, to the contrary, the United States Constitution said that Indian tribes had to be treated as foreign nations; the states had no authority over them. The question was hotly debated by newspapers and politicians.

By this time, it was clear to everybody involved that

Col-lee, a chief of the Cherokees who lost their land in Georgia, painted by George Catlin at the time of the removal.

President Jackson was not going to do anything for the Indians against the states, regardless of what the Constitution said. But when the case came up to the Supreme Court, the masterful chief justice, John Marshall, ruled that the Cherokee were not a foreign nation, but "a domestic dependent nation," and therefore the Court could not rule on the issue. Many historians today say that Marshall was clearly wrong on this point, and that the federal government, not the states, had the right to deal with the Indians. But apparently, John Marshall felt that if he ruled for the Indians, Jackson would refuse to enforce the ruling, as would certainly have been the case. The prestige of the Supreme Court would have been damaged.

However, a year later the Court, in *Worcester v. Georgia*, was confronted with the issue again, this time in a case that would be hard to duck. Many missionaries had been living with the Cherokee in order to convert them to Christianity and to teach their children white ways. The state of Georgia feared that these missionaries were also encouraging the Indians to stand up for their rights. The Georgia legislature passed laws to keep the missionaries out of tribal areas. Two of them refused to leave. They were arrested, tried, and sentenced to four years in jail. They appealed to the Supreme Court, again saying that Georgia could not pass laws affecting the Indians. This time the Court switched its position and threw out the Georgia laws. The Indians were overjoyed by this triumph, but their joy was short-lived, for Jackson refused to enforce the Supreme Court ruling against the Georgia Government. Jackson believed that the Constitution was a "white man's document" and did not apply to Indians.

By this time it was clear enough to the Indians that they were beaten and would have to go. During the early 1830s, one tribe after another signed agreements with the United States government. These agreements usually paid the Indians some money for the lands they were giving up and set aside for them large areas beyond the Mississippi River, mostly in what came to be known as Indian Territory, a large area just north of Texas, mainly in what are now Oklahoma and Kansas. Much of this land was bleak and barren.

Through the early 1830s, tens of thousands of Indians trekked west, often in parties of several thousand. These trips were frequently made in the dead of winter, with the Indians always short of food and sometimes actually starving. One farmer saw a group of Choctaw walking wearily by his farm in winter. They had two rivers to cross, both deep and cold. The farmer said:

> This they had to perform or perish. . . . This, too, was to be done in the worst time of weather I have ever seen. . . . a heavy sleet having broken and bowed down all the small and much of the large timber. And this was to be performed under the pressure of hunger, by old women and young children, without any covering for their feet, legs, or body except a cotton underdress.

Those Indians who did not want to leave their ancestral homes east of the Mississippi were driven out by force. "Families at dinner would be started by the sudden gleam of bayonets in the doorway, and rose to be driven with blows and oaths along the weary miles of trail. . . .Men were seized in their fields, or going down the road, women were taken from their [spinning] wheels and children from their play." In one party of fifteen thousand Indians traveling those weary miles, some four thousand died along the way. No wonder the Cherokee trek west was called the Trail of Tears.

Could anything have been done to spare the Indians this pain? We have seen earlier how forces like technological improvements and attitudes that sweep through a people can change history. The invention of the steamboat, the spinning jenny, the cotton gin certainly brought mas-

The Seminoles of Florida resisted efforts to remove them from the Everglades. Some of the women killed their own children to free themselves to fight with the men. Seminole resistance was successful, so their chief, Osceola, or the Black Drink, as painted by Catlin, was invited to negotiate with the American general in charge. At the meeting, he was put in chains and carried off to prison, where he died, according to the legend, of a broken heart.

sive changes to America, and so did the aggressive, expansive mood in the nation—to say nothing of the universal racism that prevailed—during the period we are examining.

But historical forces work through human beings. If the American people had reelected John Quincy Adams instead of switching to Andrew Jackson, many things might have been different. Adams probably would not have shoved the Indian removal policy through Congress as Jackson did—there was, after all, a great deal of popular opinion against it. Adams was as great a nationalist as any president and might well have sent an army to Georgia to enforce the Supreme Court's ruling and thus allowed the Indians to stay on their ancestral lands—or at least delayed and perhaps softened their removal. Adams, also, might not have pushed through increases in the protective tariff against southern wishes, and sectional divisions that led to the Civil War might have slowed. We can never know for sure how things might have turned out.

But Andrew Jackson's aggressive stance was more in tune with the American spirit of the moment than was the more cautious approach of John Quincy Adams. We must remember, when we see how Andrew Jackson's personality affected history, that the American people chose him to lead them.

BIBLIOGRAPHY

For Students

Coelho, Tony. *John Quincy Adams*. New York: Chelsea House, 1990.

Klausner, Janet. *Sequoyah's Gift: A Portrait of the Cherokee Leader*. New York: HarperCollins, 1993.

Meltzer, Milton. *Andrew Jackson and His America*. New York: Watts, 1993.

Wetzel, Charles. *James Monroe*. New York: Chelsea House, 1989.

For Teachers

Cole, Donald B. *The Presidency of Andrew Jackson*. Lawrence, Kan.: University of Kansas Press, 1993.

Davis, David B., ed. *Antebellum American Culture: An Interpretive Anthology*. Lexington, Mass.: D. C. Heath, 1979.

Pessen, Edward. *Jacksonian America: Society, Personality, and Politics*. Homewood, Ill.: The Dorsey Press, 1969.

Schlesinger, Arthur M., Jr. *The Age of Jackson.* Boston: Little, Brown, 1945.

Sellers, Charles. *The Market Revolution: Jacksonian America, 1815-1846.* New York: Oxford University Press, 1991.

Taylor, George Rogers. *The Transportation Revolution, 1815-1860.* New York: Holt, 1951.

Wallace, Anthony F. C. *The Long Bitter Trail: Andrew Jackson and the Indians.* New York: Hill & Wang, 1993.

Walters, Ronald G. *American Reformers, 1815-1860.* New York: Hill & Wang, 1978.

Watson, Harry L. *Liberty and Power: The Politics of Jacksonian America.* New York: Hill & Wang, 1990.

White, G. Edward. *The Marshall Court and Cultural Change, 1815-1835.* New York: Oxford University Press, 1991.

Page numbers for illustrations are in **boldface**.

JAMES LINCOLN COLLIER is the author of a number of books both for adults and for young people, including the social history *The Rise of Selfishness in America*. He is also noted for his biographies and historical studies in the field of jazz. Together with his brother, Christopher Collier, he has written a series of award-winning historical novels for children widely used in schools, including the Newbery Honor classic, *My Brother Sam Is Dead*. A graduate of Hamilton College, he lives with his wife in New York City.

CHRISTOPHER COLLIER grew up in Fairfield County, Connecticut and attended public schools there. He graduated from Clark University in Worcester, Massachusetts and earned M.A. and Ph.D. degrees at Columbia University in New York City. After service in the Army and teaching in secondary schools for several years, Mr. Collier began teaching college in 1961. He is now Professor of History at the University of Connecticut and Connecticut State Historian. Mr. Collier has published many scholarly and popular books and articles about Connecticut and American history. With his brother, James, he is the author of nine historical novels for young adults, the best known of which is *My Brother Sam Is Dead*. He lives with his wife Bonnie, a librarian, in Orange, Connecticut.

DATE DUE

DEC 1 5 2002	
NOV 3 0 2000	